Six Busy Days

The Wonderful Story of Creation

WRITTEN BY MARY E. ERICKSON

ILLUSTRATED BY
DAVID ACQUISTAPACE
AND
N. C. GARY

Chariot Books
David C. Cook Publishing Co.

Dedicated to
my four-year-old granddaughter, Meghan Rene,
a constant reminder of God's marvelous creation

Chariot Books is an imprint of David C. Cook Publishing Co.
David C. Cook Publishing Co., Elgin, Illinois 60120
David C. Cook Publishing Co., Weston, Ontario

SIX BUSY DAYS

Designed by Jill Novak

First Printing, 1988
Printed in USA
97 96 95 94   7 6 5 4

All Scripture quotations taken from *New International Version*.

Library of Congress Cataloging-in-Publication Data

Erickson, Mary E.
  Six busy days.

  Summary: A retelling of how God created heaven and earth in six days.
  1. Creation—Juvenile literature. 2. Bible stories—O.T. Genesis. [1. Creation. 2. Bible stories—O.T.] I.
Acquistapace, David, 1956- ill. II. Gary, N. C., 1958- ill.
III. Title.
BS651.E78 1988   222'.1109505   88-11803
ISBN 1-55513-699-0

But God made the earth by his power;
   he founded the world by his wisdom
   and stretched out the heavens by his understanding.
For he is the Maker of all things,
   . . . the Lord Almighty is his name.
                         Jeremiah 10:12, 16b

"You alone are the Lord.
You made the heavens,
   even the highest heavens,
   and all their starry host,
   the earth and all that is on it,
   the seas and all that is in them.
You give life to everything,
   and the multitudes of heaven worship you."
                         Nehemiah 9:6

*L*ong, long ago, before the beginning of time, God made the heaven and the earth. He made them out of nothing.

Heaven was a beautiful and happy place. God the Father, Jesus the Son, and the Holy Spirit lived there. The angels lived there, too.

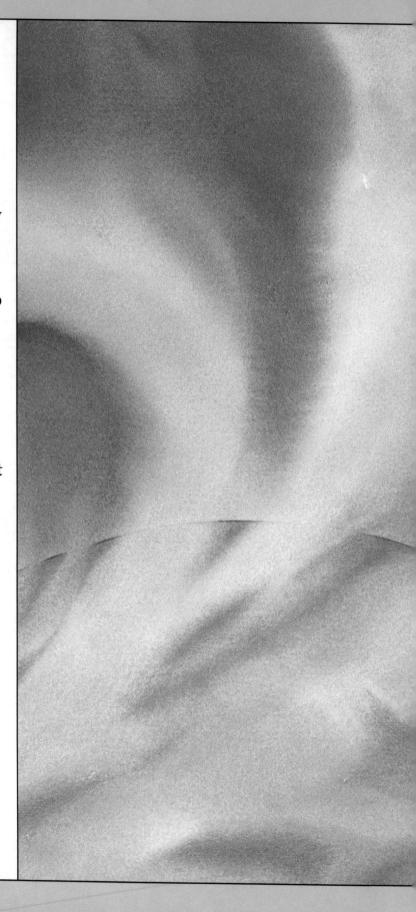

*B*ut the earth was a cold, dark, empty place. Nobody lived there.

So God decided to make the earth a beautiful place, too. He decided to make new things, things that had never been created before.

God could do that because He is all-powerful. He can do anything He wants to do.

On the first day of creation, God spoke these words: "Let there be light."

Suddenly light appeared. Some of the darkness was gone. God knew that all light would be just as bad as all darkness. God is wise.

"I'll call the light *daytime*," said God. "I'll call the darkness *nighttime*."

Then God said, "That's good!"

On the second day of creation, God looked at the earth. There was too much water. It covered everything.

So God spoke, and a blue sky appeared. The sky was filled with pure air and white clouds.

On the third day of creation, God said, "There's still too much water. There should be some dry ground."

So God just spoke. When the water separated, dry ground appeared.

God looked at what He had made. He said, "That's good! I'll call the dry ground *land*, and I'll call the water *seas*."

Then God created many kinds of land. He made brown and black soil, and white and tan sand. He made red and yellow clay, and rocks of every color.

But there was nothing growing on the earth.

So God said, "Let the earth become alive with green grass, plants, and trees."

Suddenly there were forests of tall pine trees and round shade trees. Tiny purple, pink, and blue flowers dotted the forest floor.

There were green grassy meadows covered with crimson clover and yellow daisies.

There were jungles thick with umbrella like plants and shiny green vines. Large, brilliant flowers grew beneath them.

There were deserts speckled with bushy sagebrush and thorny cactus plants. And God put flowers even on these prickly plants.

There were valleys full of fruit trees: apples, oranges, peaches, and pears. On the hillsides grew walnut and pecan trees loaded with nuts.

There were fields full of berry bushes and vegetable plants.

God smiled and said, "Ah-h! That pleases Me. I like what I have made."

Into each plant and tree, God tucked a miracle. He gave each plant a seed of its own, so His creation would live on and on.

What a wonderful and wise plan!

On the fourth day of creation, God said, "I need a bright light to rule the day. I need soft lights to shine at night."

So God set the sun in the sky to warm His world. The sun would help the plants grow. It would set the time for the days, months, and years. The sun would control the four seasons: spring and summer, autumn and winter.

God made the moon with its silver light to brighten the night. Into the blackness He scattered billions of sparkling stars. God gave each star a name.

God was proud of His lights. He smiled and said, "Ah-h! That pleases Me. I like what I have made."

On the fifth day of creation, God looked at his sky and seas. He thought, *They need to be filled with living things.*

So God spoke: "Waters, be filled with fish. Skies, be filled with birds."

Suddenly the seas, lakes, and rivers were full of fish. Large fish, small fish. Long fish, short fish. Bright fish, dull fish. Creatures too strange to imagine; creatures too colorful to describe.

*S*uddenly, in the sky, birds were flying high. Eagles flew over the mountains. Sea gulls flew over the oceans.

Some birds were flying low, like whippoorwills in the wheat fields and hummingbirds in the meadows.

Each one had a song to sing. God had thought of everything.

God watched the fish in the sea and the birds in the sky. He smiled and said, "Ah-h! That pleases Me. I like what I have made."

God blessed what He had created. He tucked a miracle seed inside each bird and fish.

"Now," said God, "you will have babies. And your babies will fill the seas and skies now and for years to come."

On the sixth day of creation, God looked at His new world. The waters were filled with fish. The sky was filled with birds. But there were no living creatures on the land.

Then God said, "Let there be animals on the earth."

And it happened. In the wink of an eye, it happened. The earth was filled with every kind of animal.

Playing in the grass were dogs and cats. Living in the desert were coyotes and curious pack rats.

Hiding in the bushes were rabbits and skunks. Up in the trees were squirrels and chipmunks.

Sheep grazed in the meadows, while bumble-bees and butterflies sucked nectar from the flowers.

Horses pranced in the pastureland, and cows drank from cool streams.

oaming in the jungles were elephants and monkeys, lions and giraffes.

Climbing the mountains were deer and elk, goats and bears.

Sunning on sandy lakeshores were tiny turtles and giant dinosaurs.

As God watched His animals, He smiled and said, "Ah-h! That pleases Me. I like what I have made."

God blessed the animals and tucked a miracle seed inside each one so they could reproduce their own kind. There would be many babies: colts and calves, cubs and kittens, pups and piglets.

What a wonderful and wise Creator!

*F*rom the heavens, God looked down on all that He had created.

"It's good," God said, "but My work is not finished yet."

And God the Father said to Jesus the Son and the Holy Spirit, "I will make man. I will make him in My own image. I will put him in charge of all that I have created."

God took some clay from the ground. With gentle, loving hands, He shaped the body of a man. God gave the man a mind so he could wisely use all the things God had made. God gave the man a soul so he could worship the Heavenly Father.

Then God breathed life into the body, and the man became a living person. God named the man Adam.

And God said, "That's good! That's *very* good!"

God watched Adam for a while.

"It's not good for the man to be alone," God said. "He needs a friend and helper."

Then God caused the man to fall asleep. From his side God took a rib, and from the rib He made a woman.

God was very pleased with the woman He had made. So was Adam. Adam named the woman Eve.

"I'm putting you in charge of everything I have made," said God. "You must think of a name for each plant, tree, bird, fish, insect, and animal, and take good care of everything for Me."

God continued, "Adam, you and your wife are My greatest creation. I have put a miracle seed inside each of you, so you can have baby boys and girls, just like yourselves."

Adam put his arm around Eve.

"When your babies grow up," God explained, "they will have babies. Someday my world will be full of beautiful people: brown and yellow, black and white. Each will be created in My image."

Now God looked at all His creation. It was perfect in every way.

God smiled and said, "Ah-h! That pleases Me. I like everything I've made."

On the seventh day, God rested from the great work He had done.

God blessed the seventh day and said, "This Sabbath day shall be a holy day."

Down through the years, God's people have rested on the Sabbath day. They rested and they worshiped God, the great and wise Creator.